THINK, WRITE, PRINT

UNWRITTEN

WORDS

An Inspired Manuscript Writing Guide from Beginning to End

Giselle Ogando

MEET THE CREATIVE COACH

Giselle Ogando is a Paterson, NJ native who currently lives in South Jersey with her amazing husband and three beautiful children. In June of 2018, with the help of her accountability partner, she launched her blog for women, She Speaks Wisdom 2 and published her 1st book, <u>Armed and Purposed: 5 Principle Truths to Discover Your Purpose.</u>

From stepping out of her comfort zone, she was able to help a couple of friends with their books. In faith, Giselle left her job; and, on October 17, 2019, she started Ready Writer Services LLC. RWS LLC is a writing, editing, and translating services company whose mission is to help others in their literary journey regardless of their experience level. Now, Giselle has helped many others step out in their writing, publish their books, and accomplish their goals!

> **When I hear a person say, "I've wanted to write this book since 2010, 2013, 2014..." And, I help them get it done. That just blesses me!**
>
> Giselle Ogando
> Ready Writer Services LLC

Contents

Intro

Some people think writing is hard. They think that they should have some type of degree in writing or journalism or to, at least, have passed a spelling bee or two in grade school. There is no way someone who can't spell can be an author, right? Or, how about someone who is phonetically challenged? There are people who love to write but believe they can't write a book. Then, there are people who have a story to tell, but don't like to write. Or, what I usually hear, "I'm not a writer." I believe this workbook was placed in my heart to dispel all the challenges people believe are keeping them from writing, publishing, and earning additional income.

I love writing. For as long as I could remember, I have loved putting words together, sharing my imagination with others, and creating new thoughts or ideas. I am a creative soul; I know that about myself. However, you might not be. That is quite alright. It doesn't mean you can't write a book. It just means, you need to know who you are with regard to writing your manuscript. But, let me ask you. Can you tell a story? Do you have a message? Do you know something others need to know? If you answered yes to any of these, you can write a book.

UNWRITTEN WORDS can be classified as a writing workbook, but I like to think of it as a living, breathing, working document that will guide you and meet you where you are in your literary journey. I know that it will help get what is "unwritten" in your head written on paper. Follow the guide, trust yourself, and let your pen be the paintbrush on this blank canvas of endless possibilities. My first tip for you: Don't overthink it, trust the process, and JUST WRITE.

Workbook Instructions

Welcome! I'm excited & grateful for your decision to use this workbook to guide you on your manuscript-writing journey! This book comes with instructions, but feel free to go at your own pace. It was created to fit a 7-week course because 7 is the number of completion. However, whether you take seven weeks or more, just make sure you commit to completing it and walking in your writing destiny! Enjoy!

Week 1: Complete Part 1 –

A. Goal-setters; B. Vision is Everything; C. So, You Want to Write?

Week 2: Complete Part 1 –

D. The Secret to Writing; E. Time Value; F. Pre-writing Do's and Don'ts

Week 3: Complete Part 2 –

A. What's the Big Idea? B. Stick to the Message; C. Do the Research; D. People, Descriptions & Feelings

Week 4: Complete Part 2 –

E. Developing Your Outline; F. Let It Flow

Week 5 & 6: Continue with Part 2, Section F. Let It Flow

Week 7: Complete all of Part 3: A through E

But, before you start, answer this: Why are you doing this? Why do you want to write this book? Never forget your why.

_____

_____

_____

_____

_____

_____

Part 1: Think

"Without reflection, we go blindly on our way, creating more unintended consequences, and failing to achieve anything useful."
Margaret J. Wheatley

Part 1: Think

A. Goal-setters

You might get a little mad at me here, but the term *goal-setters* is just that. Someone who sets goals. Nothing crazy, nothing fancy. But I will say this: Don't be a goal-setter!

I know what you're thinking! 'Say what, now?' Did I confuse you? Did I just say not to set goals? NO! That's not what I said, at all. Don't be a goal-setter. Instead, I challenge you to be a goal-GETTER! Be someone who achieves your goals! And, if you're going to achieve them, you MUST set them. And, set them, we shall (continuously).

But first…some resources/tips:

When I first started setting goals, I realized I needed to know *how* to do that. Brian Tracy, Best-selling author, speaker, and Goals Guru, wrote an amazing book titled (you guessed it), GOALS! I highly suggest you read it.

I'm a firm believer that goals are attainable when they're made visible. Whatever is your goal, put it in your face! When I published my 1st book, Armed & Purposed: 5 Principle Truths to Discover Your Purpose; I had weekly goals that I hung above my desk. For my 2nd book, Winning in Your Vows, I cut a picture of the cover and put it on my vision board. See it, believe it, achieve it!

Today, to accomplish my daily (short-term) goals and long-term goals, I use an app – Goals Wizard by Brian Tracy. No, he's not paying me to promote him. I just go with what works for me. Check the app out, if you're like me and would rather watch Blue Bloods than finish your writing project. And, the real people said…

Of course, methods vary. In my corporate life, I used the SMART plus 3 method as well. Ultimately, you must do what works for you and communicate these goals to someone who'll continually ask you about them. (My children are great at this).

On to GOAL-SETTING & GETTING!

GOALS: Write down Specific, Measurable, Attainable, Realistic, and Time-oriented goals for each. Give yourself stretch goals, not "watered-down" goals. You're better than you think you are. And, be honest with yourself; no beat-up sessions.

What is your start date goal?

_____

What is your deadline goal for your 1st manuscript draft?

_____

What is your overall writing goal regarding number of words? How many pages do you want your manuscript to be?

_____

_____

Think about your start date and your deadline. Now answer these:

My goal is to have 5 pages done by: _____
My stretch goal is to have 15 pages done by: _____
My stretch goal is to have 25 pages done by: _____
My stretch goal is to have 40 pages done by: _____
My stretch goal is to have 55 pages done by: _____

My goal is to have my title, chapter titles, and/or cover ideas by:

_____

My goal is to have my final manuscript draft to an editor by:

_____

Did I achieve my goals? Do I need to go back and rework them?

"Goals give you that sense of meaning and purpose, a clear sense of direction…. Every step you take toward your goals increases your belief that you can set and achieve even bigger goals in the future." Brian Tracy, <u>Goals</u>!

B. Vision is Everything

Whenever I start working with a client, I ask the same question. What is your vision for your book? Most of the time, I get a long pause followed by, "I have to think about it." Which is not a problem so long as you think. It's only a problem where there is never vision. See, I think most people want to write a book and start writing their book, but they don't see beyond that. And, you might be thinking, 'Well, I don't have anything written yet. How am I supposed to have a vision for it?' Great question!

Most well-run companies and organizations have planning sessions, think tanks, vision-casting, or strategic planning workshops. These exercises & events are done with the end in mind, first. In my past corporate life, we held yearly business planning meetings. During these meetings, we'd plan for budgets, goals, employee acquisition and retention, and customer engagement. But it always started with the end first, then we'd work our way back.

Vision is the power of seeing or anticipating what will be or will come. Why is vision everything? Because of the power that lies in the connection between your eyes and your mind. Don't believe me? Have you ever wanted to purchase a specific type of car in a specific color? Then, suddenly, while you're driving your old car, you start seeing that dream car everywhere you go. There is power in vision. Why do you think vision boards are so popular? Certainly not for the arts and crafts; and the sparkly purple glitter & tiny pieces of paper that get stuck onto your dining room table. Casting vision works!

Let's vision cast right now.

You have written your book, and it's published. You're promoting it on all social media outlets, and you've planned your book launch. What does that look like? And, if money and other resources were not a factor, think about what else you would or could do with your book. In the lines below, write your vision for your literary project. Examples: Would it go into schools, churches, or business organizations? Would it become a movie or a play? Would you use it to coordinate conferences or book speaking engagements? (Remember that money, connections, time & other resources are not a factor).

_____

_____

_____

_____

_____

_____

_____

_____

_____

_____

_____

_____

_____

_____

_____

_____

_____

_____

You wrote your vision. Great! Now let's try this again, but this time, consider your resources – money, time, marketing abilities, people, etc. What changed from your vision? Did you eliminate anything?

If you did, I want to offer you this. It wasn't your resources that limited your vision. It was your lack of belief in the vision. See, having vision alone is not enough. You have to believe the vision you have for your book, regardless of resources or people's opinions. I'm not saying it will always and automatically manifest. Manifested vision takes work. All I'm saying is that if you're not bought into your vision, no one else will buy it either. Vision is everything.

"The only thing worse than being blind is having sight but no vision." Helen Keller

C. So, You Want to Write?

Anyone who knows me even a little bit, knows I love self-reflection. I get a lot of clients who say they want to write, they want to write a book, they want to become an author; but that's as far as the conversation goes. Why?

It's been my experience that people who say they want to do something, usually, don't follow through unless someone (like me) is constantly reaching out. I have no problem following up a few times but, after 3 calls, if you're still pushing and delaying, then you don't want it as bad as you thought. And, no one can want it for you more than you!

So, you want to write? Why do you want to write this book? Reflect on your why (on page 6). What would finishing this manuscript mean to you? Write your answers below.

_____

_____

_____

_____

_____

If I told you I guarantee your book will be a success, generate additional income, get you speaking engagements, and change your life and (more importantly) the lives of others; what would you sacrifice? Your favorite Netflix series? Weekend nights out with friends? Hours of scrolling through social media? Think about the sacrifices you'd make; write your answers down.

_____

_____

_____

_____

_____

Can I share a secret? I love playing Toon Blast on my phone, and I'm very good at it! But I realized that, if I wanted to take my business further, I needed to sacrifice. If I wanted to be more productive, I needed to be disciplined.

Discipline is simply training or teaching yourself to do a specific thing or behave a specific way for a specific purpose.

Yes, we all love that word *purpose*. We were all created with purpose and for a purpose, but it doesn't just come to us. We must develop a discipline towards attaining it. A singer knows his/her purpose in life is to create music for others to enjoy. However, lyrics don't write themselves; musical notes don't put themselves together; and the singer's voice doesn't just hit those notes – not without discipline!

Let's stay with the singer a minute. To be effective in his or her purpose, the singer must train (discipline) him/herself to understand music notes, read the notes, and sing the notes correctly in a song, right? And, I'm willing to bet they train in their practice time, technique, and knowledge of their craft. Whatever that might look like for them, they do it.

But you must know and be honest with yourself to get the best discipline results. You must know your strengths & areas of opportunity. For example, I know that I am most productive earlier in the day, so my work schedule starts in the morning. I know that I need to continue building my business, so I follow up with potential clients weekly on Tuesday and Thursday nights. I know that I'm also a wife, a mom, a daughter, a ministry leader – I have other life "stuff" to do, so I use an app to organize my "to do" list daily. I've trained myself to do these things and get things done.

Think about your most productive times, good/bad habits, strengths & opportunities. Now look at our definition of **discipline.** Write down what disciplines you need to establish or develop in order to accomplish your writing goals. Maybe it's in your time management, organizational skills, knowledge of your topic, or getting yourself to just sit & write?

_____

_____

_____

_____

_____

_____

_____

D. The Secret to Writing

I had a client in my 90-Day Coaching program who, at our very first session, said to me, "I'm not a writer." To which I replied, "That's fine. But can you write?" She laughed and nodded in agreement. Well, 2 & a half months later, she had completed her manuscript draft. Three weeks after that, it was published! She was amazed with her accomplishment. What she thought she could not do, she did. Tell me, can you put words on paper?

Writing is marking or typing letters and words onto paper or in digital form. Is that too simple? Well, it's that simple. And, it needs to be because anything more would deter a "non-writer" from writing their story or book. Just because you're not a "writer" doesn't mean you can't write. There's a difference.

And, for my writers – yes, writing is an art. I love writing and I consider it an art because it brings out my creativity and my passion for words. However, let's consider this: most people are not Pablo Picasso, yet that doesn't stop them from grabbing paint and a paint brush, and going to town! And, if you are a writer, you must also love reading. They go hand in hand, like breathing in and breathing out.

The secret to writing is that everyone can do it! The only difference is that some of us do it more often and with a different sense of passion and purpose.

How about you? Reflect on what you've just read. What revelation did you get on whether you are a writer or someone who can write? Either way, you can and should be encouraged to pursue your goals of writing your manuscript.

_____

_____

_____

_____

_____

_____

_____

Many times, people stop writing (or never start) because they're focused on everything else except writing itself. It all stems from fear. Fear of rejection, fear of not having readers, fear of people's opinions, fear of making grammatical mistakes, fear of failure, fear of not doing it right, fear of sounding ridiculous on paper, fear of actual success, etc. Let's confront these fears/hindrances right now. You cannot conquer what you won't confront. On the lines below, write a list of hindrances preventing you from writing your book. **Use one line for each one you list.**

_____

_____

_____

_____

_____

_____

_____

_____

_____

Got your list? Now, I want you to go back up to your list and, on the left of each hindrance, write the words "Even if." Then on the right side, write "I will keep writing." **Say your revised list out loud.**

Here's a tip: Every time you start doubting yourself, your dreams of becoming an author, or your ability to write; refer to your "revised" list. In my 90-Day Coaching Program, one of the wisdom nuggets I offer my clients is to just write, and not think about who will read it or if they'll like it. Your first draft is just that – a draft. And, most of the time, your manuscript will serve you before it serves a purpose for anyone else.

E. Time Value

There are various definitions for the word, *time*. However, for right now, we can use the definition according to Merriam-Webster Dictionary that is most appropriate for this section of the book. And, although this may be the formal definition of time, we will also explore the meaning of time.

Time is an appointed, fixed, or customary moment for something to happen, begin, or end; a suitable moment.

Before I get into this topic, which is so near and dear to my heart, let's do an exercise. Below there is a list of daily activities; in the line across from each activity write down the percentage of time you spend doing it each day. The total sum of the percentages should equal 100%. **Be honest.** There is no condemnation, this exercise is meant to encourage self-awareness.

DAILY ACTIVITY	% OF TIME SPENT
Working =	_____
Eating full meals =	_____
With family/friends =	_____
Sleeping/Resting =	_____
Reading books =	_____
Exercising =	_____
Writing =	_____
Talking on phone =	_____
Watching TV/streaming =	_____
Scrolling on social media =	_____
Shopping/Online shopping =	_____
Other/Doing nothing =	_____
TOTAL =	100%

Did you notice anything glaring?

We saw the formal definition earlier, but time has a different meaning for everyone. For me, time is a precious commodity that is gifted to me and, therefore, I have the responsibility to use it wisely and productively. The older I get, the more valuable my time becomes and the more I use it to accomplish my tasks. And, the less time I have to waste! Time is more valuable than money because money comes and goes, but once time goes, you can't get it back. Think about what time means to you. How do you use it? Write your thoughts below briefly.

_____

_____

_____

_____

You might ask why reflecting on your use of time is helpful to writing your manuscript. Well, we discussed earlier that writing a book is more about discipline than writing. And, if you're not disciplined with your time, you will not finish your manuscript draft. That is a fact.

Here's a tip: To help manage my time & schedule, I plan my week the Sunday prior. I review my schedule daily & set alarms on my calendar for important stuff only. If anything unexpected comes my way, I just readjust my time. Prioritize your day and, for every task, ask yourself: how high on my list is this task? Does it ABSOLUTELY need to get done today? There are also productivity timers like the Miracle Time Cube that help with time management. Do what works for you!

Usually, I set detailed weekly writing schedules with my clients. However, because this is a bit different and I can't check up on you; we're just going to work on setting a basic 30-day schedule that I hope will give you a start to managing and MAKING time to write.

When you're thinking about the days/times you will take to write consider the first exercise we did in this section (breaking up your time into percentages). Be willing to cut down on counterproductive activities and contribute time to writing. Again, how badly do you want to finish your manuscript? Let's get scheduling.

My 30-Day Writing Schedule

Mon	Tues	Wed	Thurs	Fri	Sat	Sun
Mon	Tues	Wed	Thurs	Fri	Sat	Sun
Mon	Tues	Wed	Thurs	Fri	Sat	Sun
Mon	Tues	Wed	Thurs	Fri	Sat	Sun

Here's a tip: Make your schedule realistic to your life. In my experience, it's not that my clients don't have the time to write, it's that they don't make use of whatever time they do have. For example, if you have certain days that contain more free time than others, you should schedule writing time on those days. It can be 2-3 hours on those specific days. You don't have to write EVERYDAY! (Unless you're in a season of writing). However, if this is not your case & you're truly busy every day, then maybe 30 minutes to one hour of writing each day would work better for you. Bottom line – SCHEDULE WRITING! **And, take into consideration your goals from page 8**.

Bonus tip: For my people living with family (i.e. spouses, kids, parents, siblings…did I mention kids?), communicate your schedule! You don't have to tell them you're writing a book and will become the next Max Lucado or J.K. Rowling. But you should tell them that there will be certain times in which you will be unavailable because you're working on a project. PERIOD.

Note: The next page has additional scheduling charts in case you want to continue to schedule yourself past 30 days.

"You will never find time for anything. If you want time, you must make it." Charles Bruxton

Additional Writing Schedules (Optional)

Mon	Tues	Wed	Thurs	Fri	Sat	Sun
Mon	Tues	Wed	Thurs	Fri	Sat	Sun
Mon	Tues	Wed	Thurs	Fri	Sat	Sun
Mon	Tues	Wed	Thurs	Fri	Sat	Sun

Mon	Tues	Wed	Thurs	Fri	Sat	Sun
Mon	Tues	Wed	Thurs	Fri	Sat	Sun
Mon	Tues	Wed	Thurs	Fri	Sat	Sun
Mon	Tues	Wed	Thurs	Fri	Sat	Sun

An Encouraging Word

Time is significant but it's also a sensitive subject. I launched my blog, published my 1st book, and started Ready Writer Services LLC at the age of 35. I don't say this to brag. In fact, I've often felt like I wasted so much time in my life, and I'd kick myself for it. Any time we look back on our time spent, we run the risk of feeling defeated because of all the time that has passed. However, I want to encourage you in this matter regardless of your age or season in life. Whether you're fresh out of high school or nearing retirement, stay encouraged.

Everything that seemed like a waste was truly not a waste. Every job I've had, position I've held, and previous business venture I've started has taught and prepared me for this moment. The same goes for you. I can't tell you how many people say they've been working on their manuscripts for the past 5 years, 9 years, or 14 years! That might be you, but I'm going to tell you the same thing I tell my clients – when you finally make the decision to commit to writing your book, the time is always redeemed. Now, I'm a Christian, and I firmly believe God can stretch the time because I can tell you stories in my life where I've seen Him do it.

If you're looking at this section in remorse because of time wasted, don't! Don't focus on the time that has passed, there's nothing we can do about that. Rather, focus on the upcoming minutes. What will your time look like going forward? I've seen people write their books and publish them in as little as one month, others may take a little longer. Everyone's manuscript is different, but the key is to make good use of the time you're given to complete it.

F. Pre-writing Do's & Don'ts

We are almost ready to start writing! But before we do, I have two very important lists to give you. As you're writing, here are a few points I give all my clients. A list of what to do and not to do during your literary journey toward completing your manuscript! Do not disregard your list. Trust me, you'll need it at some point of your path. We all do.

DO...

1. Write! Just write.
2. Set a schedule
3. Use <u>one</u> source for your writing project – i.e. notebook, computer, tablet, this workbook, etc.
4. If you're using a computer, stick to one writing software – i.e. google docs, Microsoft Word, Wattpad, etc
5. Carry a small notebook with you or use the apps on your phone for sporadic thoughts
6. Know your genre(s) & stay there
7. Know your target audience
8. Get accountability (whether it's a person or writing group)
9. Set a deadline!
10. Research what you're writing about
11. Make mistakes. That's how you learn.
12. Keep writing!

Having seen the "DO's" list, write down the top three you need to focus on during your manuscript writing process. What will you do to stay focused with the ones you picked?

_____

_____

_____

_____

_____

DON'T...

1. Stop writing!
2. Get Discouraged.
3. Focus on the reader or who will read/buy your book.
4. Use illustrious fancy verbiage.
5. Worry about grammar/spelling – that's what editors are for!
6. Skip the process of getting an editor!
7. Overthink your writing.
8. Criticize your writing skills.
9. Question yourself.
10. Quit!

On the lines below, write down which "don'ts" you need to intentionally conquer the most. How will you do it?

_____

_____

_____

_____

_____

Part 2: Write

"The pen is the tongue of the mind." Miguel de Cervantes

Part 2: Write

A. What's the Big Idea?

Now that you've set your writing goals, cast vision, learned the "secret" of writing, increased the value of your time, and set your writing schedule; you're ready to start writing! So, what's the big idea?

An **Idea** is the main thought or suggestion of a topic in your manuscript. The sum of everything you've written. What are you trying to say?

Genre a specific category under which a literary work belongs.

To get here, we're going to discuss your genre, what your book is about, and who your target audience is (age category). You could be called to write different types of books or one specific genre. It's important to understand what you are writing and why you're writing your manuscript. It's imperative that you identify these so that you find your niche & your message.

What is your genre? Is it a non-fiction or fiction? I.E. children's book, a faith-based book, a devotional, a novel. Describe your book below.

_____

_____

_____

What is your book about? Is it your life story? Is it about someone else? Is it inspirational? Who are you writing this book for? Who is your target audience/age category? Jot down your answers.

_____

_____

Why are you writing this book? What do you want readers to get from it? Entertainment, information, encouragement, etc?

_____

_____

_____

_____

_____

B. Stick to the Message

Whether you're writing a testimonial or a romance novel, or even a devotional; there's something you're trying to get to your reader. Regardless of the type of book you're writing, there's always a message. So, stick to your message. DON'T DEVIATE! What do I mean?

Message, according to dictionary online, is a verbal, written, or recorded communication sent to a recipient who cannot be contacted directly.

I couldn't have defined it better myself! You cannot go to each reader and tell them directly what you're trying to tell them through your book. Your book has to be able to communicate clearly and with precision for you. Your book is your opportunity to tell them what you want them to have from your book.

Your message should be clear, candid, concise, authentic, encouraging, and wholesomely entertaining – as best as you can! Don't drive yourself crazy about your message, either. Those who need it, will receive it. Believe me.

Here's what your message shouldn't be...

- Confusing
- Contradicting
- Counterproductive
- Irrelative
- Vague
- Questionable
- Defamatory
- Harmful
- Misleading

Why did I list those? Let's say your book is about a trial or struggle in your life that you've either learned from or have overcome. Now you want to share with others so they can be encouraged. But you start writing about someone who has wronged you and was the cause of your struggle. Well, now the message about overcoming is thwarted by the wrongful things this person did. Now, the focus is on the person rather than the message.

Let's say you're writing a devotional on drawing closer to God. But you make mention that you don't need to go to church. And, you don't say anything else on that. Well, that contradicts the Bible. It also creates confusion because, while going to church isn't the "be-all and end-all" of drawing closer to God, it is part of relationship building with Him. It is one of the ways to learn more about Him. So, sometimes, we'll write something that makes sense in our minds, but is vague and creates uncertainty for the reader.

One more: let's say you're writing a fiction novel about a guy who meets a girl and falls in love with her, but they can never be together due to circumstances. Regardless of the ending, your message needs to stay the same. It's either about hope or about hopelessness. But going from hope to hopelessness, back to hope and then back to hopelessness is going to frustrate your reader. Now, if you like to be frustrated as you're reading, then go right ahead and do that. But most readers want to read without anxiety attacks.

And, please note, I'm talking about your overall message. Not to be confused with plot twists! A **plot twist** is a technique that introduces a radical change in the direction or expected end of your story. Key word being story, not message! Plot twists are typically used in fiction; although, if we're honest, a few of us have had life events happen which contained real-life plot twists!

Think about your message. What are readers around the world going to get from your book? What is the takeaway you want to give your readers even after you've left earth? Write it down and make it clear and authentic.

_____
_____
_____
_____
_____
_____
_____
_____
_____

"That's the thing about books. They let you travel without moving your feet." Jhumpa Lahiri

An Encouraging Word

Before we get into the next section, there's something else I need to make sure you get here...

Your message is yours! Own it! I hear a lot of people say, "Well, there are a lot of these types of books." Or, "My story is similar to this one." It's natural for us to downplay what's in our minds, our ideas and thoughts. We think that because something has been said before by someone else, no one will want to hear it from us. Yes, it's true that a similar message or story may have been told by someone else; but the one you have hasn't been told by YOU. You are the key. So, do not get discouraged by similar books. You didn't write those.

Your book has your name on it & your words in it. There-in lies the difference!

Right now, there is someone saying, "I wish I could find a book where I could escape reality. I just want to imagine myself on some other planet fighting to save earth." Someone else saying, "I need a book that can help me with my daily walk with God. I'm struggling" There's another person thinking, 'I just need someone who's going to be real about the struggles of poverty, someone who knows what it feels like to go through foreclosure and live on the street; and they can teach me how they came back from it.' Then, there's a parent saying, "I just wish there was a book with characters and a family my children can relate to. A book that my kids can see themselves in and be inspired by."

This right here isn't meant to pressure you, it's meant to propel you. I didn't plan on writing it, but I need you to understand that someone out here needs your book, your story, and your message. On the lines below, write the names of those counting on you for this book (the ones you know) and then list the people counting on you whom you do not know. Let this motivate you.

_____

_____

_____

_____

C. Do the Research

Whenever I'm working on a manuscript, I find myself doing more research than anything else, especially if I'm ghost writing. Research is not just for term papers. If you're going to write a good manuscript, you need to do your research; regardless of the genre, age category, or format.

Research is the investigation and study of materials and sources in order to establish credibility in a literary work.

If I wrote a book about my childhood and I grew up in the 80's, and I said I used to watch cartoons every Saturday morning on our large flat screen TV; you would know that was inaccurate because the first large flat screen wasn't sold to the public until the late 90's.

Regardless of the genre, research helps credibility and it helps your message. We might think we know plenty about the subject matter, but research will help impact your readers. For example, you may have overcome cancer and now you want to share that with others. While many will want to know your story, many more will want to know what you did and how you did it. They want to know resources and things they can use as well because they might be either fighting cancer themselves or know someone who is.

Maybe you're writing a children's book about a fictional group of kids who've known each other since Kindergarten, and one of the friends is moving away. You might need to research how kids react to life changes, how parents approach that type of news, or how kids react to losing one of their friends and how they cope. Your manuscript must be realistic and authentic, research is necessary.

But…

(yes, I'm about to make a U-turn) research is not do or die! See, research is important; but, let's be honest, you're not working on your thesis here and you're not getting graded on your manuscript. Doing research is always great but burying yourself in research is not. And, it will delay the process and prevent you from just writing. Too much research takes the art and creativity out of manuscript writing. So, keep a healthy research balance.

D. People, Descriptions & Feelings

This section is going to be a little lengthy, so we're going to divide these three topics although all throughout any manuscript, they go together like horse & carriage…and whatever third thing goes with that; blinders maybe?

Anyway, what I love the most about writing is the opportunity to use your imagination any way you want. It's exciting to know you can build people, enhance descriptions, or change feelings all within the pages of your literary work. In honing these three items, you will expand your reader's mind to meet you at your page!

PEOPLE

And, just so I don't confuse anyone; when I say build people, I do mean characters. However, I also mean people, real-life people. I'm talking about the people directly or indirectly involved in your life (past, present, and future.). Here, we're going to discuss building a fictional character/person first, then we'll talk about real people. But, for both, we're referring to the definition of character from www.dictionary.com.

Character is a person in a novel, play, or movie; also, the mental and moral qualities distinctive to an individual.

Your fictional character needs to be as real as the living people in your everyday life. This character should have a fitting name, unique physical features, a memorable personality, and a background story. They can also have an accent, depending on your story. When building a character, you should be mindful of their prescribed ethnicity, background, current environment, and written future (where you're taking your character). Science fiction leaves a lot of room for imagination, but other novels might have to be more tailor-made.

For example, if I'm writing a novel about a teenage Spanish boy growing up in Washington Heights, New York who was born in 1998. I'd most likely make his origin either Puerto Rican or Dominican. Why? Because those two were predominant cultures in that area. I might name him, Alberto Guzman; but everyone calls him "Beto" for short. Then, I'd make Beto have short, curly black hair, cinnamon brown skin, and deep brown eyes. I'd give him a mom named Hilda and a dad named Alfonso. Let's stop a minute. Do you want to know more about Beto? Me too! But do you see how Beto tied together into his ethnicity, his current community, his traits, and his family? Your character should make sense with the rest of the story.

As you build your character, you get to know them more. Their likes and dislikes. Their habits, good or bad. Their joy and sadness. It's amazing what you can do with a character when you start with the basics. Let's do that. On the lines below, build you character. Is it a female or male? Where is he/she from? Where does he/she live? What is his/her name? How old is he/she? What else about them? Even if your book is not fictional, try this. Expanding the imagination helps in all genres.

_____

_____

_____

_____

_____

_____

_____

_____

Fun right? You can write anything on the canvas of your imagination.

Now, if you noticed, there are two parts to the definition of character. The first, we'll to relate to our fictional people. The second, we can use for our real people. So, let's say your book is nonfictional. No problem. There may still be people you will have to write about depending on the type of book you're writing. And, with this, you have an even greater responsibility. It is the responsibility of being sensitive to this individual's character (mental and moral qualities).

Let's say I'm writing a testimony about my marriage and the struggles we went through. Well, I must be careful not to make my husband (or even myself) look like a horrible human being – whether we're still together or not! If you're writing about yourself or someone else, you have to choose your words wisely so as to not defame, shame, or speak ill of someone – even if it is all true! It's not your job to "unmask" a person's ugly, ugly people do that on their own. It's our job to take the high road. You might be thinking, 'But, if it's true, what's wrong with that?' The problem is that, when you allow a person's character to be tainted, your book goes from being a testimony to a "tell-all." And, your message gets lost in the juicy details of gossip. You must consider your list of readers from earlier (especially the ones you know). Everyone will have access to your book, including the person you might be writing about. So, when writing about people in your book, there are ways to position situations and say things that will not purposely tarnish another person.

Here's an example to help you see the difference in the message:

"During a board meeting, the church leader openly discussed the stigma he placed on me and whether my membership should be terminated. They even talked about banning me from the church. I've been shunned by former friends who initially weren't fond of each other, but magically formed their friendship through me and to hurt me. I've experienced deep hurt, but I chose to press through."

The message is pressing past hurtful experiences. And, you may or may not have caught that. But I guarantee you're thinking about that church leader and those friends. And, if you know the author, you'll try to speculate who these people are. The point is, your reader will spend more time thinking about the "who" than the "what." Let's try this again...

"The stigma given by former leadership resulted in the possibility of terminating my membership and banning me from the church. I've experienced rejection and mistreatment from others who shunned me, as well. See, in the past, I have experienced deep hurt by some closest to me. However, it was my choice whether or not I'd let the past affect my future."

See the difference? I talked about my experiences, but I didn't give enough detail for you to dwell on my past. Now, you can focus on my message more.

DESCRIPTIONS

Description is representing a person, object, or event in a particular way.

I love movies. In fact, I have a "stubs" membership at the movie theater, and I earn rewards every time I go to the movies. (Don't judge me). But I'm also a visual person; so, when I watch movies, it's like I'm there. I enjoy seeing the details of places, costumes, and people. Still, as visual as most of us might be, nothing beats the most powerful tool in your mind – imagination. Since most books don't have pictures, detailed description is the next best thing. If you perfect this category, you can literally lead your reader anywhere.

Description of people, places, or things is also important because it helps the reader foresee certain things in your book. Description makes it possible for you to give the readers an idea of something without straight up telling them. Whether your manuscript is fiction or nonfiction, description helps because there is no big screen to help you. So, let's practice being descriptive!

In these next few exercises, I'm going to give you a person, a place, and a thing. Rewrite each sentence with detailed descriptions that will help your reader understand more about the person, place, or thing.

The woman threw on clothes and drove over the bridge to get to work on time. How would you paint a better picture to help the reader imagine this woman heading to work? Hint: consider what time of day it might be or what type of work.

_____
_____
_____
_____

Town Pointe Park always had the best festivals. Everyone loved taking their kids there. How would you help the reader imagine the park? Hint: consider what could make this place suitable for festivals and what type of festivals?

_____
_____

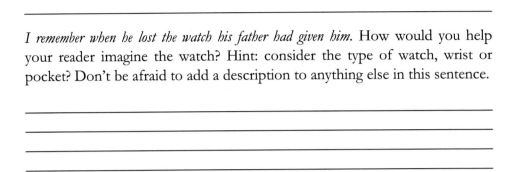

I remember when he lost the watch his father had given him. How would you help your reader imagine the watch? Hint: consider the type of watch, wrist or pocket? Don't be afraid to add a description to anything else in this sentence.

As you're writing your manuscript, don't be afraid to push the envelope a little and add descriptions of people, places, and things. Help a reader out! Then, push the envelope a little more…and add description of feelings!

FEELINGS

Here we go! This is right in my wheelhouse! When I worked in the bank, I had a manager (a really great one) who said I needed to work on my emotions because I was "very passionate and I wore my heart on my sleeve." Well, to him I say, "Thank you very much sir because now my heart pumps my purpose and drives my business. Now, I get paid for feelings!"

Feeling (for the purpose of this book) is the art showing an emotional state or reaction in your writing.

Now, I know I could've coupled descriptions with feelings, but where's the fun in that? "Feelings" needs a section all on its own. There's so much you can do to describe and invoke emotion in your readers regardless of your genre. I've read books that made me cry, made me laugh, made me get a warm fuzzy feeling in my belly, or made me want to punch a wall. I felt what the author felt. I felt what the character felt. And, I remembered their book for it.

"I've learned that people will forget what you said, people will forget what you did, but people will never forget how you made them feel." Maya Angelou

For this section (only this section), let's get all up in our feelings!

Below are a few example sentences, on the corresponding lines, rewrite and/or add to each sentence to display deeper emotion or reaction.

I didn't want to get up. Everything was dark. I just felt like pulling my covers over my head.

_____

_____

_____

She ran to Greg from the parking lot. She was so excited to see him. Greg welcomed her with open arms.

_____

_____

_____

Billy's mom and dad surprised him with a new puppy. The puppy wagged his tail when he saw Billy. Billy named his new puppy Spots.

_____

_____

_____

_____

I felt so angry. I would talk, and it was as if I wasn't even in the room. I thought, 'What more could I do to get her attention, to get my mother's love?'

_____

_____

_____

_____

Our wedding day was perfect. I had a mixture of emotions. I cried and laughed. I was so thankful to God for my husband.

_____

_____

_____

_____

_____

Emotions and reactions in detail tug at the reader's heart. It can also make a huge impact in their lives because, at some point, everyone has felt anger; sadness; grief; excitement; love; laughter; frustration; etc. Don't just write the emotion, write about what comes with the emotion – the good, the bad, the ugly. It all serves a purpose in your manuscript.

What about your manuscript? Think about your story/message. Consider your genre. What feeling(s)/reaction(s) may need to be drawn out in your writing?

_____

_____

_____

_____

_____

E. Developing Your Outline

An **Outline,** according to www.dictionary.com, is a general description or plan giving the essential features of something but not the detail.

When it comes to writing manuscripts, I like to write organically. However, outlines are important, and I have used an outline for a couple of my books. Outlines should be brief, one-page, "working" document. Details are not necessary as outlines are typically general ideas for each part of your manuscript. Below is an example for you and, on the next page, you will build your own outline. Feel free to use a pencil as you may change it a few times.

Example:

Topic: Developing a relationship with God

Target Audience: New believers. Men & women

Title: Beauty for Ashes: 60 Days with God

Intro: Who I was, what I used to believe? God was far from me. Why am I writing this devotional?

Table of Contents/Foreword – (optional)

Point A: Discovering who I am?

> 1. What does God say about me?
> 2. Who do I think I am? Different from what God says?
> 3. 20 scriptures and prayers
> 4. Journal entries

Point B: Discovering who He is?

> 1. What does the Bible say about God?
> 2. Who is He to me & how did I discover that?
> 3. 20 scriptures and prayers
> 4. Journal entries

Point C: What does God require of me?

> 1. What does God want for me and from me?
> 2. Examples of God-filled relationships

      3.   20 scriptures and prayers

This was a very basic example for a devotional. Notice there wasn't too much detail. Topics were clear and concise. The points could be chapter names or section names. Or, they can just be the topics I want to focus on as I go through each section of my devotional. This is just an outline for the real thing, a guide to keep me focused and on point, so I'm not all over the place when I'm writing. Now it's your turn! On the next page is a blank outline template.

Here's a tip: use a pencil; this is a working document which means it may (most likely will) change. Remember that it's okay to not have all the details right now but think about how you want your manuscript to flow. Don't overthink it – be general and brief. This is a brainstorming tool. The details will come as you write. Also, your book may not have chapters. It might be separated into sections or parts. That's okay, too. And, (as best as you can) try to make your outline flow in order – it will make your life easier later. Okay, time to outline! (You may not need all the lines provided).

Topic: _____

Message/Story:_____
_____

Title:

_____

Subtitle: (optional) _____

Target Audience: _____

Intro:_____

Foreword (optional)/Contents page (optional)

Chapter/section 1 topic: _____

    1. _____
    2. _____
    3. _____

Chapter/section 2 topic: _____

    1. _____
    2. _____
    3. _____

Chapter/section 3 topic: _____

    1. _____
    2. _____
    3. _____

Chapter/section 4 topic: _____

    1. _____
    2. _____
    3. _____

Possible additional Ch/sect topics & thoughts:

_____
_____
_____
_____

F. Let It Flow

This is the moment we have been waiting for! It's time to let your writing flow! Remember your do's and don'ts from Section F – Prewriting Do's and Don'ts. Right now, we're not worried about titles or sections, although you're welcome to label the pages, if it helps you. Now, we just write! Happy writing!

_____

_____

_____

_____

_____

_____

_____

_____

_____

_____

_____

_____

_____

_____

_____

_____

_____

_____

_____

_____

_____

_____

_____

_____

Hey! You are off to a great start! You made it this far, keep going!

Distractions will try to come, but remember your "Why?" Keep writing!

Wow! Look at how far you've come! You got this!

Have you checked your "Why" lately? Keep Writing!

_____

_____

_____

_____

_____

_____

_____

_____

_____

Don't worry about who's going to read it. Focus on writing.

_____

_____

_____

_____

_____

_____

_____

_____

_____

_____

_____

_____

_____

_____

_____

_____

_____

_____

_____

You're an awesome writer. Don't overthink it! Just write!

You didn't come this far, not to finish! Is there more to tell? Write it.

Part 3: Print

"If you don't see the book you want on the shelf, write it."
Beverly Cleary

Part 3: Print

A. E is for Excellence & Editing

Whenever I am at a business or an author's event, and people start talking to me about their manuscript drafts or this "book they wrote", they usually follow it up with, "Now what?" It's common for people to write something and then not know the process afterward. Especially since there are so many options for publishing now. It's overwhelming! But it pains me when writers skip the significant process of editing or rely on the publishing company's editors. A common mistake made to "save a dime". However, when you skip editing for short-term gain, you end up paying for it in other ways in the long-term.

Editing is the preparation of written material for publication by correcting, condensing, or modifying it. (www.dictionary.com)

Excellence is a standard of giving something or someone the highest quality & best effort possible even when no one is looking. Excellence is not perfection!

I promise this is not because I'm an editor (well, maybe partially), but I truly believe that editing and excellence go hand in hand. When you choose to have your written material go through an editor, you're demonstrating an expectation of high standard and quality in your work. I've heard writers state that they didn't need editing because their project was "only" a workbook or it's "only" a poem book. But no written project is "only" anything. It all matters and, if it matters and if you're going to show it to the world, wouldn't it make sense to put forth something in excellence?

So, on the next couple of pages we're going to do an exercise. Then, we'll discuss the types of editing. And, lastly, how to look for an editor – do not rely on the publishing company's editors! (Please).

Read the following paragraph. Then answer the questions below.

The Roadblocks of Life by Mr. Author

I had asked myself so many times before. Questioning is this what God wanted from me. I wasn't shore how I was going to make it it was already so had. However, their I was, sitting on my bed thinking wondering doubting however this is what God had said and I know this is where he is leading me so how can I fail? when I was younger I used to dreamed about writing. I stopped writing because life gets in the way. Its different now. It was always a dream of mine to right books and I always love reading. However, I had failed so many things what if I failed at this too? God, give me the courage to keep going. My prayer is that He will give me revelation, that if He do it for others, he will do it for me to. Irregardless of the roadblocks that come my way, I now all things are possible for him that believes.

How many times did you stop due to spelling, punctuation, or grammatical errors? _____

How many times did you have to reread a sentence within the paragraph?

_____

If you bought a book, and you saw these types of errors in it, would you want your money back? Why or why not?

_____
_____
_____
_____

Editing is Significant

Think of your book as a map that you've given your readers to lead them to a destination. Every word, every paragraph, and every page gets them closer to where you want to take them. But I submit to you, if you have errors in your book, it will make the road bumpy & confusing. You may even risk losing your reader. Even with workbooks, if your questions or exercises are worded incorrectly or your content doesn't flow, you may not get the results you're looking for. Some errors in the paragraph above might seem silly or obvious, but they're real-life, common mistakes that writers make.

As a writer/author, it's not your job to correct your writing mistakes, it's your job to make sure they get corrected. Did you get that? Your job is to write. The editor's job is to make sure what you've written is prepared for publishing. So, let's discuss the different (and most common) types of editing.

Types of Editing

    a. Copy editing – word by word editing. Involves punctuation, grammar, spelling, capitalization, and inconsistencies.
    b. Developmental/Content editing – full, in-depth type editing; flow, plot, tone. Involves critique and suggestions.
    c. Line editing – more intensive look at structure, language, flow of the written material. Fixing redundancies, vocabulary, or style.

So, how do you choose which editing is best for you?

Here's a hint: not every book will need content or line editing. However, every manuscript should be copy-edited, at least. If you're confident in your writing skills or you've had it beta read, then you may only need copy editing. If you're still on your first few drafts of your manuscript, then you may benefit the most from developmental editing. I just want you to know the differences, so you get what you pay for. Either way, editing is worth the expense.

Choosing an Editor

I'm going to give you these 7 tips for choosing the right editor.

1. Decide on the type of editing you need (not what you want)
2. Create a budget for editing – editors should tell you the fees upfront
3. It's okay to vet editors – ask for references or samples
4. Communicate your vision, timeframe, and publication goal
5. Choose an editor who is honest and understands tip #4
6. Be open to receiving feedback/critique (say, "ouch" & move on)
7. Do not rely on the publishing company's editors!

"Only a blank page needs no editing." Marty Rubin

<u>Reality Check</u>

The last four sections of this guide come after the editing and proofreading processes have been completed. However, I feel pressed to (lovingly) give you a quick reality check. I say this to my clients often because there seems to be a lot of pressure behind writing a manuscript. And, my heart is to diminish that overwhelm. So, before you look for editors, proofreaders, or beta readers. I need you to know this...

If you're still writing (or rewriting) your manuscript draft – that is OKAY! It is a draft and, most likely, your first draft of many! Writing your manuscript for your book might take one, two, or ten drafts. Do not feel bad about that! The reason it's called a draft is because there will be a final copy. I can't tell you how many times I've written and rewritten my projects.

In some cases, the editor is a huge help to guiding you with your draft. After they've done their work, you'll most likely have more to write or add into your manuscript draft. So, if you're moving into these last few sections and you're thinking you need to have your manuscript finalized to perfection, that is not the case at all. Breathe easy, stay focused, and be proud of yourself for writing your draft!

B. Is Proofreading Necessary?

What is proofreading?

Proofreading is the last stage before publishing in which a written material that has been edited is read and marked for any minor errors. Simply put, it's reading a proof of the manuscript. It differs from editing in that proofreading is not as ambitious in corrections because it's focused on surface errors. The written material should already have been edited, so no major changes should be required.

Is it necessary? Let me put it this way: before someone opens a restaurant, they typically do a soft opening. Part of the soft opening process is to put the kitchen through a "stress test". It's a method used to test the kitchen staff's ability to put out food in excellence and timeliness under pressure. I consider proofreading to be the "stress test" for written material. It's the test your work should pass before being launched to the public. So...yes. The answer is yes.

Proofreading is a paid-for service typically separate from any editing services. Some publishers may offer proofreading. Or, you can ask your editor how much they charge for proofreading, if they don't include it with their editing prices. There are many options for proofreading, however.

Here's a hint: you do not have to get your work professionally proofread, although that is good to do. However, you can have someone you trust and from whom can receive feedback to read it. Or, you can look for a beta reader.

An **alpha reader** is someone who will read your manuscript draft as it is being written from the perspective of an author.

A **beta reader** is someone who will read your manuscript/book before it is launched to the public from the perspective of the reader.

C. Who's Your Publisher?

Publishing is the act of making information available to the general public, in this case – literature.

For this section, we are going to discuss the 3 most commonly used methods of publishing. But, first, we'll briefly discuss the two different forms of publishing your book – paperbacks and eBooks.

Simply put, a paperback is a book bound in paper, it's printed. And, an eBook is an electronic book. It's downloaded and read on a device. You might think it's silly for me to review this, however (as I mentioned earlier), I've learned to never assume people know things. It's a blessing to learn something new daily.

Okay, moving on to the 3 most common methods of publishing!

1. Traditional publishing: a publisher who offers you a contract in exchange for printing, publishing, and selling your book. <u>They buy your rights</u> to publish your book <u>and pay you</u> the royalties. Some have certain content guidelines they accept. You may need to start with a book proposal, although there are some publishing companies that will allow you to submit your manuscript directly and make you an offer if they're looking for that type of content.
2. Vanity Publishing: a publisher who will publish any work of any type content so long as <u>you</u> have the money to <u>pay them</u> for their printing and binding services. The cost for their publishing may also include editing, distribution, and marketing services. They typically have publishing packages with added services. Please, please, please be careful with vanity publishers and read their offers carefully. If it doesn't make business sense – don't do it!
3. Self-publishing: when the author takes on the printing, distributing, and marketing process on their own. They take the time through different self-publishing sites in the publication of their work. It can be time consuming. However, this is, typically, the most cost-effective way to publish.

Now that you know the differences in publishing, let's do some work!

You may or may not have your manuscript fully completed – that's okay! Let's look for a publisher anyway! The next few exercises are going to require you to look up and research 3 publishing companies/resources for each method of publishing. Use an internet search engine, contact other authors, or look in the first few pages or the back of existing books you have. Research the publishing company or resource and list them below under their respective category. You can use the additional lines on the back to add any notes on any of these companies that call your attention.

3 Traditional Publishers

_____

_____

_____

_____

_____

_____

3 Vanity Publishers

_____

_____

_____

_____

_____

3 Self-publishing Sites/Resources

_____

_____

_____

_____

_____

_____

Additional Notes on Publishers/Research

_____

_____

_____

_____

_____

_____

_____

_____

Here's a tip: looking for a publisher can seem overwhelming, but it's also very exciting! Remember these few things: do your research, don't just settle, be mindful of your deadline, and count the cost with any of these three methods. Some authors like the traditional route for distribution opportunities, some may want to keep their rights to their work, others don't mind doing it themselves and saving money for marketing. Do what works best for you and always read the fine print!

Bonus tip: The two most popular self-publishing sites right now are kdp.amazon.com and press.barnesandnoble.com. If you tried to self-publish years ago, you might be familiar with CreateSpace. Well, it merged with Kindle Direct Publishing; and KDP works with Amazon. As for Barnes & Noble Press, this was formally known as Nook Press. Both KDP and Press are good, but make sure you check your royalty percentage. Again, do your research and go forth!

Copyright & ISBN

I wrestled with whether to add this in because publishers typically include this in their services. But I get asked about these two topics a lot, so I'll be brief. You can submit your own copyright application for your work. It's not complicated and can be more cost effective than having a third party do it. Get more info at https://eco.copyright.gov. You can also purchase your own ISBN (International Standard Book Number) rather than have a publisher provide it. This is the way your book is identified and allows you to sell through online and retail distribution channels. Bowker is a great resource for ISBN.

D. Mine Your *Business*

You have designated your time, set your goals, visualized your outcome. You've written, you've sought editing, you've gotten your work proofread; and now comes the fun part! It's time to *mine your business*!

Business is the investment of your time, talent, and treasure coupled with the outpouring of your passion & purpose to provide a solution to a consumer's need. This is my personal definition and testimony. I have a passion for entrepreneurship, so it is my business to tell you as an author to mine yours! Because…your book *is* a business!

(And, you should treat it as such).

I worked in retail for most of my life and when I worked at a store in the mall, I was the Merchandising Lead. It was my job to promote sales and new inventory, put together outfits, coordinate displays and update the window decals. I loved every minute of it! This is how it should be with your book. You should plan on how, when, and where to promote why readers need your book.

Every business has a grand opening or a special launch. Your book should have a launch as well. This might seem like common sense, but I have to advise it because I've had many clients tell me that the "spotlight" is difficult for them. To be honest, it's difficult for me too. I don't like to broadcast and put myself out there, but if I don't push past my comfort zone, I'm doing my purpose a great disservice. I almost made that mistake with my 2nd book. I've seen people publish a book and rather than have a formal launch, they just post it online. This will limit your success. Your book is a valuable gift to others – don't cheapen the gift!

So, we're going to talk about planning a launch party, using social media and resources to promote your book, and avenues to market you book. This section will require you to do some research! So, get your search engines ready! If you're not "tech savvy", that's okay. Just try these exercises and resources so that you are aware of all your options for mining your business (your book).

"Writing a book isn't a finish line. It's the starting gate for your career." Sean Platt

Book Covers

Every author should put thought and detail into their book cover, but you don't have to go broke doing it. I'm all about saving money while doing things in excellence. Excellence does not mean expensive! But your book cover matters. Book covers will call the reader's attention; your words will keep it! The expression 'don't judge a book by its cover' was meant for people, not books. So, I'm going to share some tips/resources for your book cover design – especially if you're on a budget.

If you're going through a publishing company, you can use their cover services. Or, you can use a graphic design artist. If you know someone who does graphic design and you can afford it, then please support small business! Go for it! If you don't know any graphic designers and you don't want to create the cover yourself, you can search www.fiverr.com for affordable graphic design artists who fit your criteria.

If you want to save marketing dollars on the cover, but still do it in excellence; you can do it yourself. It's not difficult and there are several ways to do it, especially if you're self-publishing.

1. You can use the templates that self-publishing sites like KDP or Press offer.

2. You can select and purchase images from Shutterstock or iStock, then format and add letters using Canva

3. You can use and customize the book cover templates already on Canva

Exercise #1: Think about your title and what image you would want on the front/back cover. Go to iStock or Shutterstock to browse through photos. Use your imagination! Pick the top 3 photos you like. Do not purchase the photos, this is just for simulation purposes.

Exercise #2: Go to www.canva.com and browse through their book cover category. Then, browse through their subcategories under book covers. Most are free, but do not purchase or download any. Just browse, pick one that fits your title and play around with customizing the colors, text, fonts and sizes.

Planning Your Launch

Given my culture, I love a good party! I love to see people gathered for a common cause; in this case, the celebration of your published literary art! You are a published author & you're ready to tell the world! Take your time though, plan the details, and give yourself enough time to promote your book and launch!

Here's a tip: timing is everything. Be sensitive to when you're launching your book. For example, devotionals are best to launch around December through January (Christmas/New Year) or March through April (Easter). Self-help books for weight loss would work better in the Spring/Summer than in the Winter. Finance or business books would work best in December or January. These are just examples to help you be mindful of the "when" for your book.

"Co-launches" also work well. For example, if you're launching your business and your book, your new blog and your book, or a new music CD and your book. As long as they're relevant, it's a great idea!

Selecting a venue does not have to break your bank account either. I've seen an author launch their book via a social media live video and then have an official launch at a physical location. Community centers, local bookstores, churches, hall rentals, smaller restaurants, parks (weather-permitting). Be creative and have fun with it! Most importantly, regarding date and venue – give yourself enough time to promote it!

Get someone (preferably a professional) to take pictures! You don't always have to pay, although you may want to. This is where part of your marketing dollars come in. There should be someone who can take pictures (not selfies) of you, your book, people purchasing your book, your book signing, etc. If you know someone who's on a local radio show, they may want to cover your launch as it helps them promote their show.

Exercise #3: Search for tentative book launch dates and venues. On the lines below, list your choices. Also, jot down any additional ideas for your launch, i.e. theme, colors, event duration, etc.

_____

_____

_____

_____

_____

_____

_____

_____

_____

_____

_____

Promoting Your Book/Event

There are many avenues to use for promotion. And, because we live in a social-technological era, social media marketing is currently king. There is always a platform in social media, and that should definitely be part of your marketing strategy. However, how you use social media and what you post is also important.

A book cover **mockup** is a display of your book cover in 3D images. It's like a photoshoot for your book using only the book cover image. Below is a sample of my 1st two books. These were created with only my book covers. You can use different websites to create mockups.

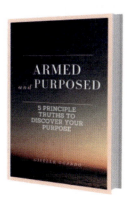 

Here's a tip: before I published my first book, I searched for book mockup sites with my sister-friend, and we came across www.adazing.com. I like using them for mockups because they have a good variety of images for great prices.

I mentioned Canva earlier when we discussed creating book covers. I love Canva, not just because of their book cover templates, but also because you can create anything with them! Posters, flyers, social media posts, sale promotional posts – anything! Which is why I will mention them again for this section. Canva is a great resource for creating posts/images to promote your book and book launch.

Exercise #4: Go to www.canva.com and browse through the different categories. Select any that are for social media posts. Then browse through the templates and pick one that you like. Customize it to announce your book and the launch date. Then click download to save it. (Most templates are free, but make sure you check the cost).

Here's an example of one I did to promote <u>Winning in Your Vows</u>…

<u>Leveraging Social Media</u>

It's rare for someone not to have some form of social media, whether it's for personal or professional use – or both. It's good to post on your own pages, but once you publish your book, you may want to create a separate page to list yourself as author or a page for your book depending on the genre and message. You might want to create a business or community page to be able to advertise through social media.

Social media groups are also very productive for promoting your book or message. For example, I had a client write about their testimony of faith in bearing children. She was told she'd never have kids and had lost three babies, yet she held onto her faith and God blessed her with three. She searched for different infant loss groups and attended those events. She was able to network before her book launch in order to promote her book. There are also author, writer, and book promotion groups you can search and join.

<u>Networking</u>

This part might be harder than the entire book writing/publishing process. Unless you're naturally a social butterfly (God bless you), this will take maximum effort because networking forces you to step all the way out of your comfort zone. But, as I mentioned before, your book is essentially your business. So, looking for and participating in networking events is crucial for the success of your book.

Your book launch should be like practice for networking. Search for local author events, author vending opportunities, book festivals, conferences (depending on your genre), and book launches of other authors. Be strategic about what events you participate in or attend. You don't need to participate in every event, but every event you do participate in is an opportunity not just to sell your book, but to meet other people who could use their authority and resources to help you.

No event is a waste! I went to a local book event and only sold 2 books, but while I was there, I met an illustrator for children's books and an author who was looking to get her book translated into Spanish to help her expand into the Spanish-speaking market. Meeting those people was more profitable than the book sales, though I was grateful for that too.

Exercise #5: Search for upcoming author events, book festivals, bookstore events (i.e. Barnes & Noble or local), conferences, etc. Make sure to filter the events that would be suitable for you given the type of book you're writing. Jot down the dates, locations, and cost to participate (if applicable).

_____

_____

_____

_____

_____

_____

_____

E. To Whom Much is Given

After you have published your book, it is your responsibility to continue "mining" and networking. I never get tired of saying that it is a business. And, I am a witness that to whom much is given, much is required. So, you cannot let this gift fall by the wayside. But I would be remiss if I didn't mention another form of stewardship that comes with the publication of your book – your finances!

Prior to entrepreneurship, I worked in retail banking for ten years. So, the banker in me cannot end this book writing process without mentioning the money. Not just the money you <u>will</u> profit from book sales, but also the money you spend in mining your business. It is your responsibility to manage the money that comes in and goes out concerning your book. So, here's what I suggest:

- Create a spreadsheet for profit and expenses (simple, not complicated)
- Track all your expenses (receipts, invoices, vendor fees, bank fees, etc.)
- Take some form of electronic payment (i.e. paypal or square)
- Record every book sale (dollars)
- Record every unit sold (books – some books you might gift to people)
- Keep track of the miles you drive to & from events

I know what you're thinking. 'All this, really?' Yes! Once you become an author, your profit from books is considered self-employed income and is not taxed. So, your expenses will also be very valuable around tax season!

Here's a tip: do not go crazy with the money from your sales! Be a good steward of your increase – tithe, save, sow into other people or projects, invest back into your book/business (marketing). Create an expense budget that includes marketing and your personal spend. On the next page, there's a profit & expense page that you're welcome to use, but you can also create your own.

"The master said, 'Well done, my good and faithful servant. You have been faithful in handling this small amount, so now I will give you many more responsibilities. Let's celebrate together!" Matthew 25:23 (NLT Bible)

Revenue Tracking

Book units sold: _____

Book sales ($): _____

Other related income: _____

Expense Tracking

Book cover: _____

Additional graphics: _____

Illustration (if applicable): _____

Marketing materials: _____

Social media marketing: _____

Editing, proofreading: _____

Launch venue: _____

Supplies for launch: _____

Event fees: _____

Bank fees: _____

Book printing: _____

Misc. _____

Net Profit: _____

Here's a tip: if you don't want to mix up your personal finances with your book sale profits, you can apply for a tax i.d. number (an EIN number) with the IRS. You could list yourself as a Sole Proprietor and open a separate business account at your bank. Now, I am a writer, not an accountant. I worked in banking not accounting. So, before you do this, check with your accountant and your state requirements regarding EIN's and business formations.

Dear future author,

I used to think publishing a book would be impossible. I used to think that I couldn't afford to publish a book. I used to think about what I would write, who would want to read it, and what if no one cared? I was so deep in my head I was getting in my way. Then, God spoke to my heart. He said, "Just write. Let Me worry about the rest."

But I want to encourage you! Regardless of whether you are just getting started in the writing process or at the tail-end of publication, keep pressing! Someone needs your book! Don't worry about who, just know they exist. And, know that they will be impacted. You have everything you need already on the inside. So, just write!

Giselle Ogando

Ready Writer Services LLC

Services:

Writing – Ghost Writing, 90 Day Coaching, Speech Writing, Writing Workshop*

Editing – Copy editing, Content editing, Proofreading

Translating/Interpreting – Spanish

Step by step self-publishing

*See schedule for writing workshop dates

Follow us: on Instagram @readywriterservicesllc or Facebook https://facebook.com/readywriterservicesllc

Contact: Giselle Ogando

Email: info@readywriterservicesllc.com

Call: 856.431.4341   Web: www.readywriterservicesllc.com

Made in the USA
Middletown, DE
19 September 2019